# FIRST AID for YOUR Emotional Hurts

Edward E. Moody, Jr., Ph.D.

## Helping Children with Learning Problems

randall house

First Aid for Your Emotional Hurts
Helping Children with Learning Problems



Published by Randall House
114 Bush Road
Nashville, TN 37217
Visit www.randallhouse.com



13-ISBN 9780892656639

Printed in the United States of America

# HELPING CHILDREN WITH LEARNING PROBLEMS

*And in every matter of wisdom and understanding about which the king inquired of them, he found them ten times better than all the magicians and enchanters that were in all his kingdom.*

*Daniel 1:20*

The Bible indicates in Daniel 1 that Daniel, Hananiah, Mishael, and Azariah were ten times brighter than their peers. How did they become that way? As one reads the passage they are left to wonder if these young men were naturally smart. However, a perusal of the book of Daniel indicates that these men seemed to attack the challenges they faced differently than their peers. In Daniel 2, the Bible indicates that the king had a dream that no one could explain to him. While others responded "there is not a man on earth who can meet the king's demand," Daniel asked for time so that he might show the interpretation to the king.

Many years ago Stanford Psychologist Carol Dweck was conducting research with 10 year-old children. She confronted them with very difficult puzzles. She noted that some of the children encountered the puzzles and said, "I love a challenge." Another confronted a hard puzzle and said, "You know I was hoping this would be informative." This experience led her to delve into the mindsets of people about learning and intelligence. She found that there are two types of people, those who believe intelligence is fixed and those who believe intelligence grows. Her research indicates that those who believe intelligence is fixed make few efforts to grow (since one can do little about their situation). On the other hand, those with a growth orientation will attack a challenge, learn from it and grow as a result.[1] In this booklet we will argue from a growth perspective. This is especially important if you have a child that struggles with learning difficulties.

Many children struggle with learning as well as attention and hyperactivity problems that impair their ability to succeed in the classroom. Perhaps you have a child with a problem like this and are struggling to help them. Maybe you find yourself confused about how to help. You are not alone.

- 5-8% of youth suffer from Attention Deficit Hyperactivity Disorder (ADHD).[2]
- 7 out of every 100 school children have ADHD.[3]
- It is estimated that 5-15% of youth have a specific Learning Disability (LD).[4]
- The school dropout rate for children or adolescents with LD's is reported at 40% or approximately 1.5 times the average.[5]

Learning problems, left unaddressed, can result in lifelong difficulties. There is a cascading effect with one problem leading to another. For example, a child who struggles to pay attention can quickly find himself getting into trouble at school. Soon his grades may suffer. Difficulty paying attention and staying on task can lead to difficulty learning.

- 44% of children with ADHD have at least one other disorder.
- 20-25% of children with ADHD have learning difficulties.[6]

These problems can result in a child feeling ostracized in the classroom and experiencing multiple peer problems. Eventually these difficulties can impact earning potential and important life decisions. The longer these problems continue, the more likely they are to lead to further problems.

Students who have learning problems may feel isolated from their peers that can lead to negative feelings like shame, anger, and low self-esteem. At times the classroom struggles a child experiences may impact how peers view them leading the child to become more susceptible to being bullied. The negative attitudes and actions of others can have a detrimental effect on the behavior, social relationships, education, future employment, and long-term health of the student. For example, students diagnosed with LDs are at greater risk for social maladjustment and involvement in risk-taking behaviors (e. g., suicide, substance abuse, sexual activity) than their peers without a disability. Some students with an LD develop poorly defined self-concepts and low self-esteem.[7]

*Train up a child in the way he should go; even when he is old he will not depart from it.*

*Proverbs 22:6*

Whatever the difficulty the child you are working with may be facing, it can be better when you have a growth perspective. The Scriptures instruct us to train our children. Your child may not learn in the same way as other children but they will benefit from solid training.

Sometimes as you try to help a child with ADHD or an LD you may be impeded by those who say, "I never heard of that when I was growing up." However, those who have spent much time around people from previous generations will note that many people never finished school. At times this was because of the financial circumstances like the Great Depression. However, it is unlikely that many of the children who suffer from learning problems today would have continued in school had they been part of a previous generation. A walk through history will show there is nothing new about these problems. We know by examining the work of many figures from the past that a large number of people have suffered from learning problems throughout history.

**Famous people who appear to have had learning or attention problems**[8]

| | | |
|---|---|---|
| Beethoven | Alexander Graham Bell | Winston Churchill |
| Walt Disney | Thomas Edison | Albert Einstein |
| Dwight D. Eisenhower | Henry Ford | Galileo |
| Danny Glover | John F. Kennedy | Carl Lewis |
| Mozart | Louis Pasteur | Gen. George Patton |
| Eddie Rickenbacker | Nelson Rockefeller | Charles Schwab |
| George C. Scott | George Bernard Shaw | Sylvester Stallone |
| Lindsay Wagner | Robin Williams | Woodrow Wilson |
| Henry Winkler | Wright Brothers | Leonardo da Vinci |

This list spans centuries showing there is nothing new about these difficulties. Additionally, the prominence of these individuals indicates that a learning problem does not relegate a child to a future dominated by failure. Our goal in this booklet is to teach you about the particular problem your child may experience so that you will be in a better position to help them. You will also learn about ways to utilize specialized services for the child. Finally, we will encourage you to take a growth approach with the child you are trying to help by providing specific activities you can use to help them.

**ADHD through History**[9]

- 1890—William James describes an "explosive will"
- 1902—George Still lectures about attention symptoms
- 1950-1970s—"hyperactive child syndrome" emerges
- 1968—"hyperkinetic reaction of childhood" is described
- 1987—"Attention-deficit hyperactivity disorder" listed is the Diagnostic and Statistical Manual of Mental Disorders-Third Edition (DSM-III)

## What is ADHD?

An ADHD diagnosis is typically made at age 6 when a child begins formal schooling. ADHD is characterized by impulsivity, inattention, and difficulty with executive functioning.[21]

**ADHD Problems in early elementary school**[22]

- Off-task behavior
- Incomplete or lost assignments
- Sloppy work or messy handwriting
- Errors in accuracy
- Inconsistent performance
- Daydreaming
- Disruptive behavior
- Difficulty interacting with others

## Hyperactivity

Excessive activity is the most visible sign of ADHD. Even in sleep children with ADHD are "on the go."[23]

### *Hyperactivity Symptoms*[24]

- Fidgets or squirms
- Leaves seat in situations when remaining seated is expected
- Runs or climbs excessively in situations in which it is inappropriate
- Has difficulty playing or engaging in leisure activities quietly
- "On the go"
- Talks excessively

## Impulsivity

A child with ADHD often acts without fully considering the circumstances or the consequences of their behavior. There is a "have it now attitude."[25]

### *Impulsivity Symptoms*[26]

- Blurts out answers before questions have been completed
- Has difficulty awaiting their turn
- Interrupts or intrudes on others

**Attention**

The ability of a child to exercise selective attention improves with age for most children. At the age of 4 a child is not expected to have the attention focusing skills of a 12 year old. However, for the child with ADHD, attention is a major deficit. An inability to engage in selective attention impacts school achievement and all areas of their life.[27] This problem translates to difficulty sustaining attention long enough, especially with tedious tasks, difficulty resisting distractions and maintaining sustained attention, as well as failure to pay sufficient attention, especially to details. For example, children with ADHD have more accidents and ADHD has been associated with more dangerous driving.[29] Some have hypothesized that the increase in accidents by youth with ADHD is due to poor motor coordination.[30]

> Lack of attention skills in the preschool years predicts poorer reading, spelling, and mathematics scores 8 years later.[28]

### *Inattention Symptoms*[31]

- Fails to give attention to details or makes careless mistakes
- Has difficulty sustaining attention
- Does not seem to listen when spoken to directly
- Does not follow through on instructions
- Has difficulty organizing tasks
- Avoids tasks that require sustained mental effort
- Loses things necessary for tasks or activities

- Distracted by external stimuli
- Forgetful

---

## Executive Functioning

The difficulties brought on by ADHD lead to difficulties in executive functioning (EF). EF is brain related processes needed for applying problem-solving skills to achieve goals. EF encompasses planning, cognitive flexibility, abstract thinking, the ability to follow and incorporate rules, taking appropriate actions, and inhibiting inappropriate actions.[32]

**Executive Functioning Difficulties in Children with ADHD[34]**

- Lack problem-solving skills
- Poor sense of timing
- Inconsistent
- Difficulty resisting distraction
- Difficulty delaying gratification
- Trouble working on long-term goals
- Easily frustrated
- Poor judgment

EF difficulties arise as a result of problems with concentration, memory, and cognitive organization.[33] This leads to working and retrieval memory problems in the child increasing the difficulties encountered. Working memory is the ability to keep one thing in mind while working on another. Retrieval memory involves being able to locate on demand information that has been learned and stored in memory.

**Many ADHD students also have problems with[35]**

- Time management
- Prioritizing work
- Reading comprehension
- Note taking
- Study skills
- Completing tasks with multiple steps

EF problems are evidenced in many ways. The child will have difficulty organizing and setting proper priorities that result in difficulty beginning a task. Once a task is underway it becomes difficult to sustain attention or shift from one task to another. Sustaining effort also becomes problematic as well as managing frustration and emotion.[36]

---

### Executive Functioning Problems and Descriptions[37]

| *Problem* | *Description or Example* |
|---|---|
| Difficulties with social perception | Child may be unaware of what is happening around them |
| Does not understand consequences | Pulls chair out from under another child but does not understand that child will fall on the floor |
| Difficulty expressing feelings | Trouble apologizing for actions |
| Trouble delaying gratification | Instead of asking to play or use something, may grab that item |
| Trouble listening | In conversations with others repeatedly interrupts rather than listening |
| May smile less | When playing with another child may not smile much |
| Unwilling to act | When a situation arises may be less likely to act (e.g., ask to join in with others to play) |
| Fails to ask questions | Less likely to ask questions when they do not understand something |
| Talking | Either does not talk enough or talks too much |
| Tendency to ask inappropriate questions | May ask "off the wall" and annoying questions to a teacher |

| | |
|---|---|
| Lacks interpersonal problem solving skills | May struggle with feelings of being rejected by others |

ADHD can be divided into three types: predominant inattentive type, hyperactive-impulsive type, and combined type.

### ADHD Predominantly Inattentive Type

If a female has ADHD it will most likely be this type. This individual will often appear as if they are not paying attention. The child may go from one toy to another, and is easily distracted.[38] An individual with this type of ADHD would experience six or more of the inattention symptoms for at least a six month time period.[39]

### ADHD Predominantly Hyperactive-Impulsive Type

Many young children act without thinking. However, the child with this type of ADHD routinely interrupts others and is impaired in the ability to inhibit their behavior requiring greater supervision than other children. There is great difficulty organizing schoolwork and these problems are seen in all areas of life.[40]

The hyperactive nature results in a child who is seemingly unable to play quietly. Problems with peers are seen as this child is often rejected and viewed negatively. Unsurprisingly, this type of ADHD seems to especially result in poor academic achievement and lower intelligence test scores.[41]

### ADHD Combined Type

This is the most common type of ADHD. This individual has 6 or more of the inattention or hyperactivity-impulsivity symptoms for at least a six-month period.[42]

## Assessment of ADHD

To determine if a child has ADHD it will be necessary for a licensed psychologist to conduct a thorough, multifaceted assessment. A proper assessment will consist of interviews with a parent (preferably both parents), teachers and the child. In addition, the psychologist would benefit from observing the child in a classroom setting and if possible while engaged in other activities. Parents should be prepared to provide information about their child's prenatal and postnatal development as well as medical, social and educational history. Information regarding parental style and disciplinary techniques will be helpful as well. One might begin by observing the behavior of their child and providing a concrete description of their behavior (e.g., leaves seat after sitting for only one minute) as well as what happens just before and right after the behavior occurs. To properly diagnose ADHD a helping professional should ask parents, teachers and in some cases the child to complete a rating scale.

---

**Behavior Rating Scales used to Assess ADHD**[43]

- Comprehensive Parent and Teacher Rating Scale (ACTeRS)
- ADHD Rating Scale
- Attention Deficit Disorder Evaluation Scale—School Version
- Attention-Deficit/Hyperactivity Disorder Test
- Behavior Assessment System for Children-Teacher Rating Scales (BASC-TRS)
- Child Behavior Checklist-Parent Teacher Rating Form (CBCL-TRF) Achenbach
- Devereux Behavior Rating Scale-School Form

---

A student may also be given an individually administered intelligence test (e. g., Wechsler Intelligence Test, Stanford-Binet, Kaufman Assessment Battery for Children), and an individually administered achievement test (e.g., Woodcock-Johnson Psycho-Educational Battery Test of Achievement, Wide Range Achievement Test). These instruments can provide more diagnostic information about the academic needs of the child. Later in this booklet we will look at how the results of these instruments can be used.

## What causes ADHD?

Throughout history many have hypothesized about the causes of ADHD. Causes suggested have ranged from excessive sugar to watching too much television. However, overall research has failed to support many of these hypotheses. For example, research does not support the consumption of sugar or artificial dye as a cause for ADHD. Diet has long been believed to be a cause for ADHD. However, in studies on the issue, diet restrictions have only helped about 5 percent of children with ADHD and those were children who had food allergies.[44] Watching excessive television is associated with attention problems but it is important not to confuse correlation with causation. Television use does not appear to cause ADHD. On the other hand, a lack of a structured environment may be a cause of ADHD. Research supports a link between social environment and ADHD. However, longitudinal research does not indicate that social environmental factors are solely responsible in the development of ADHD.[45]

The exact cause of ADHD is not known. However, there is strong support in the research to indicate that ADHD is inherited. For example, research has indicated that siblings of a person with ADHD are at a greater risk to develop ADHD. There is research that indicates that 25% of biological parents of children with ADHD have a history of ADHD compared to 4% of adoptive parents.[46] Studies indicate that 25 percent of the close relatives in the families of ADHD children also have ADHD.[47] Studies of twins indicate a strong genetic influence exists in the disorder[48] with a heritability rate of 77%.[49] The culprit behind ADHD appears to be the neurotransmitter dopamine. It also appears that norepinephrine is involved to some extent.[50] This has resulted in vigorous attempts to treat the problem with medication.

## ADHD Treatment

### Medication

The most commonly used treatment for ADHD is stimulant medications like Ritalin, Dexedrine, and Cylert. Stimulants are effective with 75 to 90% of children with ADHD. About 80% of children will need medication as adolescents, and 50% need medication as adults.[51] These medications enhance the neurotransmission of dopamine and norepinephrine in the brain by increasing norepinephrine and dopamine in the prefrontal cortex of the brain.[52]

> Four-fifths of ADHD youth treated with psychostimulant medication are considered responders compared to 4% to 30% treated with placebo.[53]

Stimulants, at the proper dosage, have a temporary "focusing" effect that can increase the child's ability to sustain attention, decrease impulsiveness, and improve performance on fine motor tasks and a wide range of cognitive tasks. Stimulants have been used to treat ADHD for more than 40 years. Initially these medications would wear off after several hours. Now the use of extended release forms allow for longer impact. These medications can decrease physical hyperactivity. However, these benefits do not always translate into increased academic performance.[54]

**Psychostimulant Medications**[55]

| *Trade Name* | *Generic Name* | *Typical Daily Child Dosage* | *Level of Insomnia* |
|---|---|---|---|
| Adderall | amphetamine | 5-30 mg | Moderate |
| Adderall-XR | mixed salts | 5-30 mg | Significant |
| Cylert | pemoline | 37.5 mg | Moderate |
| Dexedrine | dextroamphetamine | 5-10 mg | Mild |
| Dextrostat | | | |
| Dexedrine Spansules | | | Moderate |
| Desoxyn | methamphetamine | 5-25 mg | Mild |
| Ritalin (effective 2-6 hours) | methylphenidate | 10-30 mg | Mild |
| Ritalin-SR | | | Moderate |
| Methylin-ER | | | Moderate |
| Metadate-ER (effective 6-8 hours) | | | Moderate |
| Concerta (once per day dosing) | | 18-54 mg | Significant |
| Focalin (effective 2-6 hours) | dexmethylphenidate | 5-30 mg | Mild |

Negative effects linked to stimulant medications include unwanted side effects like anxiety, insomnia, irritability, weight loss, increased blood pressure and heart rate as well as occasional motor tics. Not all children who take the medications improve. Some stimulants may lead to suppressions of growth and height.[56] However, it appears that children who take stimulant medication may grow slower than those who do not, but their average final height does not differ.[57]

### Behavioral Interventions

Even if one utilizes stimulant medication with a child, for lasting effect other interventions will need to be utilized. Behavioral treatment includes behavioral parent training, classroom behavioral management, social skills training, and intensive outpatient/summer treatment programs.[58]

Behavioral interventions have been used to enhance the use of medication and at times have been used successfully alone to intervene with children with ADHD. These interventions involve positive reinforcement (providing praise and attention for appropriate behavior), withdrawal of reinforcement (placing a child in time-out or removing something desired when a child engages in inappropriate behavior), a point system (setting up a system of rewards and costs for appropriate and inappropriate behavior), and contracts. Contracts consist of agreements between teachers and students or a child and parent where the expected behavior is described and the consequences for inappropriate behavior made clear. The parent and child work together on behavioral goals for the child.[59]

### Cognitive-Behavioral Interventions

Cognitive-behavioral interventions have also been used to increase a child's ability to think before acting and wait for gratification. Examples of this approach include using problem-solving skills to guide ones actions and using self-monitoring techniques to keep track of appropriate and inappropriate behaviors.[60] It appears that the best treatment approach is a combination of psychological and pharmacological approaches that uniquely meet the needs of a particular child.[61]

## What can you do?

Begin by getting an evaluation of your child by a psychologist. If the child is believed to suffer from ADHD investigate the feasibility of the interventions recommended by the psychologist. Explore the use of medication with your physician. If medication is utilized closely monitor your child for side effects and progress. At times various medications and dosage amounts will need to be tried for success. Utilize the services provided by your child's school. Many children with ADHD will qualify for special education services in the public school under the Other Health Impairment section under the Individuals with Disabilities Act (IDEA). It is also possible to receive services under Section 504 of the Vocational Rehabilitation Act. This would allow a student in a public school setting to qualify for special services and interventions.[62]

### Partner with Teachers

Talk to the teacher of your child and ask that they be placed near the teacher, a student role model and in a low interruption area.[63] Prepare your child for school. Help them focus upon what the teacher will be expecting of them. If the child can exhibit key social skills their teacher will be able to more effectively help them, and the child will develop better rapport with their teacher.

---

**Social Skills Teachers Expect[64]**

- Correct schoolwork
- Ignoring distractions while working
- Completes assignments in a timely manner
- Tells teacher appropriately when mistreated by others
- Keeps clean and neat desk
- Introduces self to new people
- Controls temper with peers and adults
- Appropriate response to peer pressure and aggression from others

---

Cooperation is key in the classroom. Precious instructional time in the classroom is lost when students are disruptive or having difficulty. Below are cooperation skills teachers have rated as most important.

### Cooperation Skills Important for Success[65]

- Follows and attends to directions
- Gets along with people who are different
- Uses time wisely while waiting for help
- Listens to classmates and their ideas

## Addressing Inattention

To address problems with inattention teach attention skills to your child. Attention is a process. The key for proper attention is where the focus is placed where the focus is needed, and how the child sustains that focus. The individual must inhibit urges to focus on unimportant stimuli and to shift attention when needed.[66]

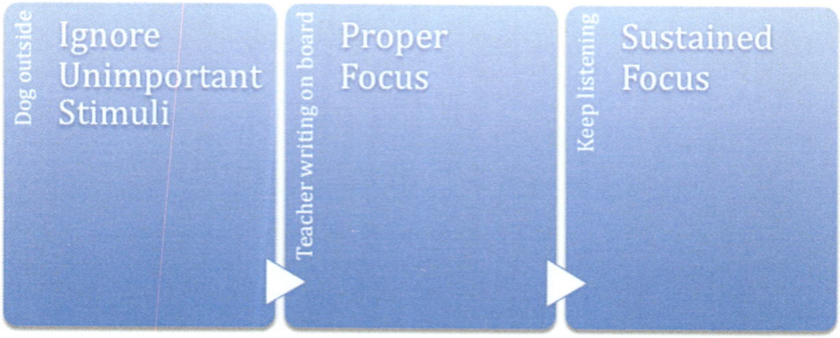


### Addressing Problems with Attention[67]

- Define the appropriate behavior expected while giving praise to the child
- Give praise immediately for appropriate behavior
- Vary the statements given as praise
- Be consistent and sincere with praise
- Ignore inappropriate behavior
- Remove nuisance items
- Provide calming manipulative

Practice attention skills as you work with your child. For example, begin by removing nuisance items from a room and then you might read a story. Praise the child for apparent attention. Praise them if they are able to answer questions about the story correctly. As you work to build attention gradually lengthen the stories or complexity of the problems presented. You may find that the child fidgets or performs some other activity as you read. If they are tracking the story ignore that behavior for now.

### Addressing Hyperactivity and Impulsivity

Some of the most annoying behaviors that children with ADHD engage in are a result of hyperactivity and impulsivity. Hyperactivity and impulsivity symptoms can be annoying to teachers, peers, and others. It is important to help your child learn how to delay gratification properly. One area to work on is communication skills. Below are skills that should be taught to the child.

---

**Work on communication skills**[68]

- Let the speaker finish
- Concentrate on what is being said
- Show interest in what others are saying
- Avoid judgment
- Eliminate putdowns
- Express agreement and use praise

---

If a child makes progress in the area of communication they will have better rapport with teachers and students. This will greatly diminish some of the negative impact of ADHD. Practice having the child listen to others to develop attention skills. Give them feedback about the eye contact they provided to the speaker. It will also be helpful to provide training in how to carry on a conversation and compliment others. For example, when trying to talk to a peer one might ask about favorite sports team, toys, pets, and games. When giving compliments one might focus on how the other person looks. The child should practice these skills, use them, and return home and describe how it went.

### Addressing Executive Functioning

Be an executive (good boss) to your child. Give the child the necessary structure they need by making expectations clear. Provide continuity by trying to do the same thing at the same time every day (e.g., snack, playtime, homework). Have simple systems for organization. Use planners and organizers to build organizational skills. Help them clean out their backpack and notebook weekly.[69]

Make a list of problematic behaviors then select three to five from the list to work on them (being respectful, doing homework, and going to bed on time).

Create a reward system, and use punishment and time-out.[70] Once the child develops a set of skills move to another problem.

It seems like there are so many problems that need to be addressed. View problems as opportunities (growth perspective). As problems arise use and teach the problem-solving steps.

---

**Problem-solving Steps[71]**

1) Define the problem
2) Come up with workable solutions
3) Implement the solution
4) Evaluate results and try something else if necessary

---

Here is how one might utilize the steps with a child. If a child is being teased at school one could define that as the problem. Once the problem is defined, steps can be taken to generate workable solutions. These solutions are evaluated and an appropriate action chosen which is followed by implementation of the solution. After the child implements the solution they should return home and evaluate the results. At times adjustments will need to be made where other solutions are generated.

ADHD can be debilitating. However, when seen as a challenge and through a growth orientation lens a child can overcome these difficulties and emerge successful. In the next section we will examine learning disabilities and address steps to take to address learning problems.

As many as 4 million U.S. school children may be suffering from an LD.[72]

Another area of difficulty that many children face is that of a specific learning disability. Learning disorders are defined as academic achievement below expectations for age, years in school, and IQ score. An LD may be diagnosed when the individual's achievement on individually administered standardized tests (e.g., like the Woodcock-Johnson) in reading, mathematics, or written expression is substantially below what is expected based on the child's age, schooling, and intellectual level (as measured by an individually administered intelligence test like the WISC). The learning problem impacts the daily life of the child in addition to academic functioning.

Many individuals with LDs (10-15%) also struggle with Conduct Disorder, Oppositional Defiant Disorder, ADHD, Major Depressive Disorder, or Dysthymic Disorder.[73]

There is a lot of variation in learning disabilities. Within reading disabilities there can be problems with word recognition and spelling as well as comprehension, and fluency. Within mathematics there can be problems with computations and problem solving. A written expression disability can consist of problems in handwriting, spelling, and/or composition.[74]

## Reading Disorder

The most common type of learning disorder is Reading Disorder, which is sometimes called dyslexia or referred to as "word blindness." The prevalence of Reading

- The prevalence of dyslexia has been estimated to be as high as 17.4% of the school-age population.
- Reading disabilities in general have prevalence estimates of 10-15% of the school-age population.
- Dyslexia is the most common form of LD.
- It is estimated that 80-90% of children served in special education programs have problems with reading.[76]

Disorder in the United States is estimated at 4% with 60-80% of those diagnosed with the problem being male.[75]

Reading Disorder is associated with reading achievement. For example, reading accuracy, speed, or comprehension as measured by standardized tests. Children with Reading Disorder may display oral reading errors like omitting words, reading slowly and failing to understand something read.[77]

There are signs that help one know if a child may be struggling with Reading Disorder. For example, there are some common spelling errors by children with Reading Disorder.

---

**Looking for spelling errors**[78]

| *Error* | *Example* |
|---|---|
| Omission of silent letters | wether for weather, reman for remain |
| Omission of sounded letter | requst for request |
| Omission of double letter | suden for sudden |
| Addition of letters | untill for until |
| Reversal of letters | was for saw |
| Vowel problems | prisin for prison |
| Consonant problems | Cecond for Second |

---

Reading disabilities in general reflect persistent deficits rather than a developmental lag in linguistic and reading skills.[79] This underlies the importance of early intervention.

---

**Signs that a Reading LD may be present**[80]

- Has trouble learning the alphabet, rhyming words or connecting letters to sounds
- Makes mistakes when reading out loud
- Repeats words and frequently pauses when reading out loud
- Difficulty understanding what one has read
- Trouble with spelling

- Trouble remembering the sounds represented by letters
- Trouble discerning the slight differences between words
- Trouble understanding jokes or sarcasm
- Trouble following directions
- Mispronounces words
- Uses a word incorrectly that sounds like another

## Mathematics Disorder

Mathematics Disorder is sometimes called dyscalculia. This involves a diminished ability to understand mathematical terms, operations or concepts. There is difficulty performing mental calculations which may lead the child to rely on other devises like counting on their fingers.[81] Mathematics Disorder is associated with mathematical ability as measured by standardized tests. Mathematics Disorder is commonly found in combination with Reading Disorder or Disorder of Written Expression.[83]

> 5-6% of school-age children are believed to have Mathematics Disorder.[82]

## Signs that a Mathematics LD may be present[84]

- Confuses math symbols
- Misreads numbers
- Gets lost in the middle of math calculations
- Reverses numbers
- Does not know multiplication/addition/subtraction facts
- Fails to regroup
- Fail to complete the problem
- Guesses
- Is careless

## Disorder of Written Expression

> 1 in every 250 U.S. children have written expression disability.[85]

Disorder of written expression or dysgraphia is more than sloppy handwriting. It includes difficulty composing grammatically correct sentences. Errors include punctuation, spelling errors and a diminished ability to organize coherent written paragraphs.[86] The essential feature of this disorder is writing skills (as measured by an individually administered test of writing skills). It is unclear about how prevalent the disorder is.[87]

---

**Signs that a LD in Written Expression may be present[88]**

- Trouble with handwriting
- Difficulty holding pencil
- Trouble expressing ideas in writing
- Started talking late
- Limited vocabulary
- Difficulty organizing what one wishes to say
- Difficulty retelling a story
- Difficulty thinking of a word one wishes to use in writing or a conversation

---

## Assessment of Learning Disabilities

The goal of any assessment is to intervene as soon as possible with a child who is struggling to achieve. A proper assessment will need to be conducted by a psychologist to determine if your child has a specific learning disability. The examiner will need to know about academic and behavioral functioning, developmental history, health history, personality temperament, and family history of learning problems. Before talking with the examiner consider whether there is anything pertinent about family, school or community that might be needed to make a proper diagnosis.[89]

The assessment process for specific learning disabilities can be confusing since different states have different requirements for how a specific learning disability is identified. Most states still allow for a specific learning disability to be identified when there is a severe discrepancy between intelligence and achievement. Twelve states have a required response to intervention approach to specific learning disability identification. The response to intervention approach is used to implement evidence-based interventions in the general education classroom with supplemental and intensive intervention.[90]

Whatever approach is used to identify the learning disability, as a parent you should look closely at the cognitive and neurological testing results of your child. Little can be known about the cognitive capabilities, processing strengths and weaknesses of a child without this kind of assessment.[91]

Below is an example of results on the Wechsler Intelligence Scale for Children. This particular student has a Reading and Written Expression LD.

**Wechsler Intelligence Test for Children**

| *Scale* | *IQ* | *Percentile Rank* |
|---|---|---|
| Verbal Scale IQ | 97 | 42 |
| Performance Scale IQ | 115 | 84 |
| Full Scale IQ | 105 | 63 |

Examination of the scores alone does not indicate the particular learning disability this child has. However, the discrepancy between the child's verbal and performance IQ (18 point spread) suggests there is a problem. In the past when I have conducted psychoeducational evaluations I have tried to explain these results to parents to help them get some context for the issue their child is facing. For example, the child portrayed above obtained a verbal scale IQ of 97 that was in the 42$^{nd}$ percentile. That means he scored as well as or better than 42% of the norming population of the WISC. On the other hand, he obtained a performance scale IQ of 115 that was in the 84$^{th}$ percentile. That means he scored

### Attention Deficit Hyperactivity Disorder (ADHD)

The problem of ADHD can be traced back to the time of Shakespeare. Shakespeare made reference to King Henry the VIII who experienced a "malady of attention."[10] Later a German poem entitled "Fidgety Phil" described a hyperactive child that would probably meet the diagnostic criteria for ADHD today.[11] In 1890, William James described an "explosive will" which resembled ADHD.[12] From the 1950s to the 1970s there was emphasis placed on "hyperactive child syndrome" and hyperkinetic impulse disorder.[13] The disorder "hyperkinetic reaction of childhood" was listed in the DSM in 1968.[14]

> - It is believed that 3,290,000 students in U.S. schools are struggling with ADHD.[15]
> - ADHD between the ages of 4 to 6 predicts academic achievement 8 years later.[16]
> - Boys are 4 to 9 times more likely to be disagnosed with the disorder.[17]
> - Roughly 3% of preschool children meet the criteria for ADHD.[18]

Around 30 years ago many assumed that children grew out of ADHD. However, one-half of the children with ADHD, and some suggest as many as three-quarters experience attention problems that persist into adolescence. Roughly 50% of ADHD cases persist into adulthood. The presence of conduct problems, oppositional behavior, and family problems increase the likelihood that ADHD problems will persist.[19] It appears that ADHD does not really go away it simply becomes less obvious after a child leaves the classroom and finds an environment better suited to their particular needs.[20]

as well as or better than 84% of the norming population on the WISC. These results point to his strengths and weaknesses, and with the help of an examiner, effective interventions could be designed and implemented for the child.

The same student was administered the Woodcock-Johnson Psycho-Educational Battery. This helped to identify his particular learning disabilities.

**Woodcock-Johnson Psycho-Educational Battery**

| *Cluster* | *Age Percentile* | *Grade Percentile* |
|---|---|---|
| Broad Reading | 23 | 15 |
| Broad Mathematics | 61 | 55 |
| Broad Written Language | 38 | 36 |
| Broad Knowledge | 42 | 41 |

Note in this example, the child scored in the 15th percentile on Broad Reading (scored as well as or better than 15% of the norming population), and the 36th percentile on Broad Written Language (as well as or better than 36% of the norming population). This allowed him to be diagnosed with Reading Disorder. Professionals who conduct assessments related to LDs should have a working knowledge of educational interventions and a relationship with professionals in or out of school.[92] The assessment should provide teachers and parents the information needed to begin addressing the child's learning problem.

It helps to have an idea about what specific IQ scores indicate.

**Making Sense of IQ scores[93]**

| *Wechsler Scale IQ* | *Classification* |
|---|---|
| 132 and above | Very Superior |
| 120-131 | Superior |
| 110-119 | High Average |

| | |
|---|---|
| 90-109 | Average |
| 80-89 | Low Average |
| 70-79 | Borderline |
| 69 and below | Mentally Deficient |

However, to intervene properly an examiner will need to go beyond IQ score and examine specific subtest scores. Ask the examiner to discuss subtest results and subsequent interventions with you.

**Making Sense of Wechsler Intelligence Test Subtest Results**[94]

| *Scaled Score* | *Percentile Rank* | *Descriptions* |
|---|---|---|
| 17-19 | 99 | Very Superior |
| 14-16 | 91-95 | Superior |
| 13 | 25-84 | High Average |
| 7 | 16 | Low Average |
| 5-6 | 5-9 | Borderline |
| 1-4 | 1-2 | Mentally Handicapped |

## What causes learning disabilities?

The cause of LDs is unclear. There is probably not a single neurological cause but an inability for certain parts of the brain to work together. Genetics appears to play a role with concordance rates of 71% of monozygotic twins and 49% of dyzygotic twins. Many children with a reading disorder also have a parent with that disorder, however reading disorders do not appear to result from the inheritance of a single gene.[95]

> 25-60% of parents of children with reading problems also display reading problems.[96]

## Learning Disability Treatment

Once a thorough psychoeducational evaluation has been conducted treatment can begin on a child with a specific learning disability. This will require the help of educational professionals, special education teachers as well as the parents and extended family of the child. Approximately 12% of students between the ages of 6 and 17 years are served under the Individuals with Disabilities Act of 2004. The percentage of students receiving services for a specific learning disability was 6%.[97] There are some general principles that will help regardless of the particular disability the child faces.

### General Treatment Principles

When a child struggles with a learning disability there is a temptation to avoid learning tasks. That temptation must be resisted and instead one must increase time on task, working on the area of concern (reading, math, or written expression). To do this you will need a well-developed and organized instructional approach that routinely involves cumulative review. Help the child develop self-regulation strategies (proper thinking about self, approach to homework). Remember, progress must be frequently monitored because the job is never done.[98]

Below are some general guidelines to help a child with a learning disability.

---

### Treatment of LD in General[99]

1. Space learning over time
2. Weave example solutions with problem-solving exercises
3. Combine graphics with verbal instructions
4. Integrate abstract and concrete representations of concepts
5. Make and use frequent quizzes to promote learning
6. Help the child allocate study time efficiently
7. Ask the child explanatory questions

---

### Utilize Assessment Results

Earlier, the results of the WISC and WJ were provided of a student who struggled with two learning disabilities. Below are the subtest results for that particular student. It will help to examine the subtest results for your child as well.

**Wechsler Intelligence Test for Children**

| *Subtest* | *Scaled Score* | *Percentile Rank* |
|---|---|---|
| **Verbal** | | |
| Information | 11 | 63 |
| Similarities | 11 | 63 |
| Arithmetic | 12 | 75 |
| Vocabulary | 7 | 16 |
| Comprehension | 7 | 16 |
| Digit Span | 13 | 84 |
| **Performance** | | |
| Picture Completion | 12 | 75 |
| Picture Arrangement | 13 | 84 |
| Block Design | 11 | 63 |
| Object Assembly | 14 | 91 |
| Coding | 11 | 63 |

For this particular child Object Assembly, Digit Span and Arithmetic are strengths while Vocabulary and Comprehension are weaknesses. The results of these evaluations are used to design interventions for particular students. However, it is important that parents utilize this information as well since they will interact far more with their child. Below are suggestions for activities parents can use to adapt to the particular needs of their child based on the subtest results.

**Addressing Particular Verbal Subtests Results**[100]

| *Subtest and Measure* | *Activities to address deficits* |
|---|---|
| Information (general knowledge) | Have the child read sections from the newspaper and summarize content |
| Vocabulary (verbal fluency and knowledge) | Develop a dictionary by identifying words the child does not recognize and placing the words in a notebook that is developed into a dictionary |
| | Have the child repeat simple stories and explain how the characters are thinking and feeling |
| | Utilize games like Scrabble |
| Comprehension (knowledge of social mores) | Get the child to develop alternate endings to stories |
| | Discuss the actions of others to help the child see possible motivations of others |
| | Talk about current events, like how the government works |
| | Role-play situations like reporting fires, calling the Police, asking for help |
| Similarities and vocabulary (measures verbal conceptual) | Utilize show and tell games and scrapbooks with classifications of things like animals, vehicles, and utensils |
| | Have children find communalities in dissimilar objects |
| | Review basic concepts such as days of the week, directions and distances |

**Addressing Particular Performance Subtests Results**[101]

| *Subtest and Measure* | *Activities to address deficits* |
|---|---|
| Digit Span, Arithmetic, Picture Completion, | Have the child arrange cards in a meaningful sequence |
| Picture Arrangement (attention and concentration) | Use mathematical word problems<br>Use tracing activities<br>Drill basic mathematical concepts |
| Block Design and Object Assembly (spatial-visual ability) | Have the child identify common objects and details<br>Use block-building activities<br>Use jigsaw puzzles |
| Coding, Block Design, Digit Symbol, Object Assembly, and Mazes (visual-motor) | Use paper-folding activities<br>Have the child solve mazes<br>Have the child draw from memory |

## Treatment for Reading Disorder

Interventions for reading disorder include developing skills necessary for phonological processing and fluent reading, with later emphasis on reading for comprehension.[102] Children with Reading Disorder tend to struggle when taking tests. You can help them by working with them to improve test-taking skills. For example, when preparing for a multiple-choice test, break down the test into three areas: studying for the test, taking the test, reviewing completed test.

### Studying for the Test[103]

- Know the main concepts
- Study details
- Practice writing multiple-choice test questions
- Practice taking multiple-choice tests
- Review prior test-taking errors

Then work on taking the test.

### Taking the Test

- Scan all test items
- Read the entire question
- Identify and use clue words
- Eliminate obviously wrong answers
- Identify difficult item
- Answer difficult items last
- Respond to each item

One is not done after completing the test.

### Reviewing Completed Test

- Review correct responses
- Identify test-taking skills used
- List possible reasons for incorrect response
- Identify test-taking errors for incorrect items
- Study incorrect items

During the summer, school breaks and other times encourage your child to read books. Ask them questions after they read a book and teach them to ask these questions to themselves.

---

**Examples of questions to ask after reading a book**[104]

1. What made the book interesting?
2. What did you like or dislike about the book?
3. Which characters in the book would you like to have as friends?
4. What else would you have liked to have seen happen in the book?
5. If you had been the main character, what would you have done differently?
6. What would you say to the author of the book if you met them?
7. What would you like to change about the story?
8. Which of the events or situations that the characters experienced have you experienced?

---

### Treatment for Mathematics Disorder

If you are trying to help a child that has Mathematics Disorder it will be important to utilize arithmetic drills and memorization skills.[105] It appears that a child with this kind of difficulty struggles often with memorization. As they work through a mathematical problem there is a tendency to forget numbers and easily become confused. A key is to drill basic mathematical concepts until they become second nature. As the child develops skills it will be important to increase the complexity of problems and to impose time limits on the completion of problems. Resources for parents from the National Center for Learning Disabilities can be found at www.ncld.org.

### Treatment for Written Expression

For written expression, first engage the child in simple writing tasks like keeping a diary and as skills improve provide more challenging tasks.[106] The bottom line is that the child must write more to improve their writing skills. Have them read stories and summarize them. Encourage them to rewrite their school notes from classes, and encourage them to develop more complex sentences. When a student struggles with handwriting have them use tracing models to produce letters. For older students have them practice by completing job applications or completing blank forms.[107]

### What you do matters

As you look at Daniel, Hananiah, Mishael, and Azariah in Daniel 1 you have to ask, "What made them different?" There was probably more to them than simply being very bright. A close examination of their lives indicates they were responsible, resilient, and possessed reasoning abilities. Their parents taught them responsibility, reasoning skills and resilience. They were responsible when they asked for an alternative to violating their conscience. They were resilient as they survived the destruction of their country and their transfer to another country. They demonstrated reasoning skills as they dealt with dictators and rival politicians.

> Although learning disabilities often persist into adulthood as a whole people with learning disabilities function well within society. The prognosis is determined by the ability to engage in creative problem solving, abilities required for different careers, age at which LD was identified, ability to set reasonable goals, access to appropriate interventions, attitude toward life challenges, effectiveness of support systems, family's attitude about the LD, peer group's attitude about the LD, teacher's attitude about the LD, and the ability to persevere.[108]

If you are a parent of a child with ADHD or a LD it is important to try to help them with some of the interventions in this book. However, the most important skills are the basic skills of responsibility, resilience and reasoning.

Three life skills that have been identified as key to raising student achievement are responsibility, resilience, and reasoning. These are skills that can be taught and learned. Possible outcomes of them are improved study skills, improved school attendance, improved relationships, collaboration, and achievement.

Responsibility involves being accountable for your own actions and inactions as well as the consequences for your actions and inactions.

---

**Levels of Responsibility**[109]

*Personal responsibility*: It is up to me to create what I want. It is up to me to make it happen. How I act matters.

*Academic responsibility*: Good grades result from my efforts. If I learn it is up to me. If I don't understand, I have to ask.

*Social responsibility*: Considering other peoples' points of views (I care about what you have to say). Concern for the common good (I care about what is good for all of us, not just for me). Giving help and seeking help (I will help you. I need help).

---

Reasoning involves thinking that utilizes explicit and/or implicit rules. The student thinks, "If I am going to think clearly about solving a problem (or reaching a goal) I need clear rules to follow."

Resilience involves competently surmounting challenges, both inside and outside of school. Challenges and difficulties are a normal part of life. We all have them.

Persistence/Determination comes down to saying, "If at first I don't succeed I will try again but I do need balance." This student views obstacles as challenges to overcome. "What can I learn from this? How can I approach this challenge?"[110]

> In one study eighth graders who watched more than 5 hours of television per night had the lowest average mathematics scores recorded in the Third International Mathematics and Science Study.[111]

As a parent or someone close to a child you can help them develop these skills. Parental involvement in school and a home focused on academics are critical influences on academic achievement. Parental involvement is also related to higher educational aspirations, motivation to achieve, lower rates of disciplinary problems, higher rates of extracurricular involvement and higher rates of school completion. When you supervise their homework, discuss school and current events, encourage them to read, screen their television viewing and peer activities, and help them learn to delay gratification and set long term goals you are putting them on a path to success.

## Resources

### Attention Deficit Hyperactivity Disorder

Children and Adults with Attention Deficit/Hyperactivity Disorder (CHADD) www.chadd.org

Attention Deficit Disorder Association (ADDA) www.add.org

Center for Disease Control and Prevention (CDC)-Attention-Deficit/Hyperactivity Disorder www.cdc.gov/ncbddd/adhd

Council for Exceptional Children www.cec.sped.org

Council for Exceptional Children (CED) Division of Early Childhood www.dec-sped.org.

Graphic Organizers for all Types of Instructional Needs www.teachervision.fen.com/graphic-organizers/printable/6293.html

HealthTalk: ADHD www.healthtalk.com/go/adhd

WebMD ADD and ADHD Health Center www.webmd.com/add-adhd

### Learning Disabilities

LdPride www.LdPride.net

Learning Disability Association www.ldonline.org

Learning Disability Association of America www.ldanatl.org

National Center for Learning Disabilities www.ncld.org

TeachingLD www.teaching.ld.org

### Writing

Handwriting without Tears www.hwtears.com

Read, Write, and Type www.talkingfingers.com

The Handwriting Worksheet Wizard www.startwrite.com

### Spelling

Franklin Spelling Tools www.franklin.com

Scholastic Spelling www.scholastic.com

Spellography www.sopriswest.com

### Composition

Draft Builder www.donjohnston.com

Excellenceinwriting www.Excellenceinwriting.com

Easy Essay www.easyessay.com

### Reading

Read Please www.readplease.com

### Math

Touch Math www.touchmath.com

## Helpful Books

R. A. Lougy, S. L. DeRuvo, and D. Rosenthal. *The School Counselors Guide to ADHD: What to Know and Do to Help Your Students.* Thousand Oaks, CA: Corwin. (2009).

G. Kewley, P. Latham. *100 Ideas for Supporting Pupils with ADHD.* New York: Continuum International Publishing Group. (2008).

## Helpful Interventions for Reading

**Read Naturally** (www.readnaturally.com) This is an approach that works on reading fluency, speed and comprehension. This program is usually recommended for a minimum of 30 minutes a day, three to five days a week.

**Great Leaps Reading** (www.greatleaps.com) Supplemental reading program that requires just 10 minutes per day, for a minimum of three days a week. The goal is to enhance reading fluency.

**Read 180 (Scholastic)** (www.read180scholastic.com) A balanced literacy program that involves interactive and adaptive software.

**Wilson Reading System (Wilson Language Training)** (www.wilsonlanguage.com) This program is designed specifically for people with dyslexia. There is immediate emphasis on the six syllable types.[110]

## References


1 C. Dweck. *Mindset*. New York: Random House. (2007).

2 P. C. Kendall & J. S. Comer. *Childhood Disorders-Second Edition.* New York: Psychology Press (2010).

3 American Psychiatric Association. *Diagnostic and Statistical Manual of Mental Disorders—Fourth Edition—Text Revision (DSM-IV-TR).* Arlington, VA:APA (2000).

4 P. C. Kendall & J. S. Comer. *Ibid.* (2010).

5 American Psychiatric Association. *Ibid.* (2000).

6 R. A. Barkley. ADHD In E. J. Marsh, & R. A. Barkley *Child Psychopathology*—2nd Ed. New York: Guilford Publications (2010).

7 G. W. Lambie & A. Milsom. A Narrative approach to supporting students diagnosed with learning disabilities. *Journal of Counseling & Development, 88* (2) (2010):196-203.

8 R. E. Cimera. *Learning disabilities: What are they? Helping teachers and parents understand the characteristics.* Lanham, MD: Rowman & Littlefield Education (2007).

9 R. A. Barkley. *Ibid.* (2010).

10 G. F. Still. Some abnormal psychical conditions in children. *Lancet, 1,* 1008-1012, 1077-1082, 1163-1168.

11 M. A. Stewart. Hyperactive Children. *Scientific American, 222,* 94-98. (1970).

12 W. James. *The principles of psychology*. London: Dover. (1890).

13 S. Chess. Diagnosis and treatment of the hyperactive child. *New York State Journal of Medicine, 60,* (1960):2379-2385.

14 American Psychiatric Association. *Diagnostic and statistical manual of mental disorders* (2nd Edition). Washington, DC: Author. (1968).

15 E. M. Rapoport. *ADHD and Social Skills: A step-by-step guide for teachers and parents.* New York: Rowman & Littlefield Education. (2009).

16 P. C. Kendall & J. S. Comer. *Ibid.* (2010).

17 P. C. Kendall & J. S. Comer. *Ibid.* (2010).

18 P. C. Kendall & J. S. Comer. *Ibid.* (2010).

19 P. C. Kendall & J. S. Comer. *Ibid.* (2010).

20 G. W. Lambie & A. Milsom. A Narrative approach to supporting students diagnosed with learning disabilities. *Journal of Counseling & Development, 88* (2) (2010):196-203.

21 P. C. Kendall & J. S. Comer. *Ibid.* (2010).

[22] R. Pierangelo & G. Giuliani. *Classroom Management Techniques for Students with ADHD.* Thousand Oaks, CA: Corwin Press. (2008).

[23] R. Pierangelo & G. Giuliani. *Ibid.* (2008).

[24] American Psychiatric Association. *Ibid.* (2000).

[25] R. Pierangelo & G. Giuliani. *Ibid.* (2008).

[26] American Psychiatric Association. *Ibid.* (2000).

[27] R. Pierangelo & G. Giuliani. *Ibid.* (2008).

[28] P. C. Kendall & J. S. Comer. *Ibid.* (2010).

[29] P. C. Kendall & J. S. Comer. *Ibid.* (2010).

[30] D. C. Beidel, C M. Bulik, and M. A. Stanley. *Abnormal Psychology.* Boston: Prentice Hall. (2010).

[31] American Psychiatric Association. *Ibid.* (2000).

[32] P. C. Kendall & J. S. Comer. *Ibid.* (2010).

[33] R. Pierangelo & G. Giuliani. *Ibid.* (2008).

[34] R. Pierangelo & G. Giuliani. *Ibid.* (2008).

[35] R. Pierangelo & G. Giuliani. *Ibid.* (2008).

[36] T. E. Brown. A new approach to attention deficit disorder. *Educational Leadership, 64* (5), (2007): 2-27.

[37] E. M. Rapoport. *Ibid.* (2009).

[38] P. C. Kendall & J. S. Comer. *Ibid.* (2010).

[39] American Psychiatric Association. *Ibid.* (2000).

[40] P. C. Kendall & J. S. Comer. *Ibid.* (2010).

[41] P. C. Kendall & J. S. Comer. *Ibid.* (2010).

[42] American Psychiatric Association. *Ibid.* (2000).

[43] R. Pierangelo & G. Giuliani. *Ibid.* (2008).

[44] R. Pierangelo & G. Giuliani. *Ibid.* (2008).

[45] R. Pierangelo & G. Giuliani. *Ibid.* (2008).

[46] P. C. Kendall & J. S. Comer. *Ibid.* (2010).

[47] R. Pierangelo & G. Giuliani. *Ibid.* (2008).

[48] R. Pierangelo & G. Giuliani. *Ibid.* (2008).

[49] D. C. Beidel, C M. Bulik, and M. A. Stanley. *Ibid.* (2010).

[50] R. Pierangelo & G. Giuliani. *Ibid.* (2008).

[51] R. Pierangelo & G. Giuliani. *Ibid.* (2008).

[52] D. C. Beidel, C M. Bulik, and M. A. Stanley. *Ibid.* (2010).

[53] R. S. Sinacola & T. Peters-Strickland. *Basic psychopharmacology for counselors and psychotherapists.* Boston: Pearson. (2006).

[54] R. S. Sinacola & T. Peters-Strickland. *Ibid.* (2006).

[55] R. S. Sinacola & T. Peters-Strickland. *Ibid.* (2006).

[56] P. C. Kendall & J. S. Comer. *Ibid.* (2010).

[57] D. C. Beidel, C M. Bulik, and M. A. Stanley. *Ibid.* (2010).

[58] D. C. Beidel, C M. Bulik, and M. A. Stanley. *Ibid.* (2010).

[59] J. M. Sattler & R. D. Hoge. *Assessment of Children: Behavioral, Social, and Clinical Foundations* (Fifth Edition). San Diego: Jerome M. Sattler, Publisher, Inc. (2006).

[60] J. M. Sattler & R. D. Hoge. *Ibid.* (2006).

[61] R. S. Sinacola & T. Peters-Strickland. *Ibid.* (2006).

[62] R. Pierangelo & G. Giuliani. *Classroom Management Techniques for Students with ADHD.* Thousand Oaks, CA: Corwin Press. (2008).

[63] R. Pierangelo & G. Giuliani. *Classroom Management Techniques for Students with ADHD.* Thousand Oaks, CA: Corwin Press. (2008).

[64] M. Beebe-Frankenberger, K. L. Lane, K. M. Bocian, F. Gresham, and D. MacMillan. Students with or at risk for problem behavior: Betwixt and between teacher and parent expectations. *Preventing School Failure, 49* (2), (2005):10-17.

[65] K. L. Lane, J. H. Wehby, and C. Cooley. Teachers' expectations of students' classroom behavior across the grade span: Which social skills are necessary for success? *Exceptional Children,* 72 (2), (2006):53-167.

[66] R. Pierangelo & G. Giuliani. *Ibid.* (2008).

[67] R. Pierangelo & G. Giuliani. *Ibid.* (2008).

[68] R. Pierangelo & G. Giuliani. *Ibid.* (2008).

[69] R. Pierangelo & G. Giuliani. *Ibid.* (2008).

[70] R. Pierangelo & G. Giuliani. *Ibid.* (2008).

[71] R. Pierangelo & G. Giuliani. *Ibid.* (2008).

[72] D. C. Beidel, C M. Bulik, and M. A. Stanley. *Ibid.* (2010).

[73] American Psychiatric Association. *Ibid.* (2000).

[74] J. M. Fletcher, G. R. Lyon, L. S. Fuchs, & M. A. Barnes. *Learning Disabilities: From Identification to Intervention.* New York: The Guilford Press. (2007).

[75] American Psychiatric Association. *Ibid.* (2000).

[76] J. M. Fletcher, G. R. Lyon, L. S. Fuchs, & M. A. Barnes. *Learning Disabilities: From Identification to Intervention.* New York: The Guilford Press. (2007).

[77] D. C. Beidel, C M. Bulik, and M. A. Stanley. *Ibid.* (2010).

[78] J. M. Sattler & R. D. Hoge. *Ibid.* (2006).

[79] J. M. Fletcher, G. R. Lyon, L. S. Fuchs, & M. A. Barnes. *Learning Disabilities: From Identification to Intervention.* New York: The Guilford Press. (2007).

[80] J. M. Sattler & R. D. Hoge. *Ibid.* (2006).

[81] D. C. Beidel, C M. Bulik, and M. A. Stanley. *Ibid.* (2010).

[82] J. M. Fletcher, G. R. Lyon, L. S. Fuchs, & M. A. Barnes. *Learning Disabilities: From Identification to Intervention.* New York: The Guilford Press. (2007).

[83] American Psychiatric Association. *Ibid.* (2000).

[84] J. M. Sattler & R. D. Hoge. *Ibid.* (2006).

[85] J. M. Fletcher, G. R. Lyon, L. S. Fuchs, & M. A. Barnes. *Learning Disabilities: From Identification to Intervention.* New York: The Guilford Press. (2007).

[86] D. C. Beidel, C M. Bulik, and M. A. Stanley. *Ibid.* (2010).

[87] American Psychiatric Association. *Ibid.* (2000).

[88] J. M. Sattler & R. D. Hoge. *Ibid.* (2006).

[89] J. M. Sattler & R. D. Hoge. *Ibid.* (2006).

[90] J. M. Fletcher, A. E. Barth, & K. K. Stuebing. A response to intervention (RTI) approach to SLD in *Essentials of Specific Learning Disability Identification.* Edited by D. P. Flanagan & V. C. Alfonso. Hoboken, NJ: John Wiley & Sons, Inc. (2011).

[91]A. S. Kaufman & N. L. Kaufman. Series Preface in *Essentials of Specific Learning Disability Identification.* Edited by D. P. Flanagan & V. C. Alfonso. Hoboken, NJ: John Wiley & Sons, Inc. (2011).

[92] J. M. Fletcher, G. R. Lyon, L. S. Fuchs, & M. A. Barnes. *Learning Disabilities: From Identification to Intervention.* New York: The Guilford Press. (2007).

[93] J. M. Sattler & R. D. Hoge. *Ibid.* (2006).

[94] J. M. Sattler & R. D. Hoge. *Ibid.* (2006).

[95] D. C. Beidel, C M. Bulik, and M. A. Stanley. *Ibid.* (2010).

[96] J. M. Fletcher, G. R. Lyon, L. S. Fuchs, & M. A. Barnes. *Learning Disabilities: From Identification to Intervention.* New York: The Guilford Press. (2007).

[97] G. W. Lambie, & A. Milsom. A Narrative approach to supporting students diagnosed with learning disabilities. *Journal of Counseling & Development, 88* (2) 196-203. (2010).

[98] J. M. Fletcher, G. R. Lyon, L. S. Fuchs, & M. A. Barnes. *Learning Disabilities: From Identification to Intervention.* New York: The Guilford Press. (2007).

[99] N. Newcombe, N. Ambaby, J. Eccles, L. Gomez, D. Klahr, M. Linn, K. Miller, & K. Mix. Psychology's role in mathematics and science education. *American Psychologist, 64* (6), 538-550. (2009).

[100] J. M. Sattler. *Assessment of Children (Third Edition).* San Diego: Jerome Sattler Publisher, Inc. (1988).

[101] J. M. Sattler. *Ibid.* (1988).

[102] D. C. Beidel, C M. Bulik, and M. A. Stanley. *Ibid.* (2010).

[103] W. N. Bender. Learning Disabilities: *Characteristics, identification, and teaching strategies (Fifth Edition).* Boston: Pearson. (2004).

[104] A. G. Kamhi & H. W. Catts. The language basis of reading: Implications for classification and treatment of children with reading disabilities. In *Speaking, reading, and writing in children with language learning disabilities: New Paradigms in Research and Practice* (Edited by K. G. Butler & E. R. Stillman). Mahwah, NJ: Lawrence Erlbaum Associates, Publishers.

[105] D. C. Beidel, C M. Bulik, and M. A. Stanley. *Ibid.* (2010).

[106] D. C. Beidel, C M. Bulik, and M. A. Stanley. *Ibid.* (2010).

[107] N. Mather, & B. J. Wendling. How SLD Manifests in Writing. In *Essentials of Specific Learning Disability Identification.* Edited by D. P. Flanagan & V. C. Alfonso. Hoboken, NJ:John Wiley & Sons, Inc. (2011).

[108] J. M. Sattler & R. D. Hoge. *Ibid.* (2006).

[109] J. Cogan & R. Wright. *The Other 3 Rs: Teacher's Manual.* Washington, DC: American Psychological Association. (2004).

[110] J. Cogan, & R. Wright. *Ibid.* (2004).

[111] R. F. Subotnik, & G. White. *The Theory Behind the 3Rs Project. In R. Sternberg, & R. F. Subotnik. Optimizing student success in The Other 3Rs: Reasoning, Resilience and Responsibility.* Greenwich, CT: Information Age. (2006).